The Air Lost in Breathing

The Air Lost in Breathing

SIMONE MUENCH

Winner of the Marianne Moore Poetry Prize
Selected by Charlie Smith

HELICON NINE EDITIONS
KANSAS CITY & LOS ANGELES

© 2000 by Simone Muench

Thanks to Jennifer Whitten, Julia Rooney, David Meihouse, and
Stephanie McCanles for immeasureable support.
Acknowledgments continued on page 85.

Cover and book design: Tim Barnhart

Helicon Nine Editions, a non-profit small press, is funded in part
by the National Endowment for the Arts, a federal agency,
the Kansas Arts Commission and the Missouri Arts Council,
state agencies, and by the N.W. Dible Foundation.

Kansas Arts Commission   MAC

Library of Congress Cataloging -in-Publication Data

Muench, Simone.
    The air lost in breathing : poems / Simone Muench.-- 1st ed.
        p. cm.
    Winner of the 1999 Marianne Moore Poetry Prize.
    ISBN 1-884235-30-1 (acid-free paper)
        I. Title.

PS3563.U358 A75 2000
811'.6--dc21

                                                            00-057564

Manufactured in the United States of America
FIRST EDITION

HELICON NINE EDITIONS
KANSAS CITY & LOS ANGELES

To Retta, Jesse, John and Reg—
for being my reason

Table of Contents

I. LETTERS TO EROS

11 Finale for a Girl in a Skirt Sewn of Sky
12 Letters from a Lover from Another Planet
13 The Fix-it Man
14 Red Dress
16 As if
17 Tom Waits, I Hate You—
19 Inflorescence
21 The Problem with Celibacy
23 Toledo Bend
25 The Air Lost in Breathing
26 Denali Highway
27 His Black Scrawl
28 The Body's Migration
30 Open Letter to Eros

II. WHEN WE BREATHE

35 Branches
36 Insomnia
38 The Jesus Apostrophes
41 Girls Gathered for a High School Photo, Circa 1960
42 Your Limbs Are Knotted Ropes
43 Blackberries
44 Love Travels in the Pockets of Old Men
45 Le roi
47 Sin
48 When We Breathe
49 Loneliness

51 Refrains in Elkins, Arkansas

52 Negative

53 It Is the Cloud-Shingled Sky that Sends Me Back
    to You

54 Bone-flower

56 On Hearing My Father Pulled a Shotgun on My
    Grandparents during Thanksgiving Dinner

58 Eating Honeybuns on the Louisiana Highway

59 Undone

III. EXHALATIONS

63 Desire Takes a Road Trip to New Orleans

65 Desire's Exhalations and the Incidentals of Happiness

67 Walking

69 Bell Peppers

71 The Etiquette of Shells

72 Arizona

73 There Is a Word for It

74 Night-Blooming Cereus

75 It is in this field

77 Reading Ed Ochester on the Plane from Chicago to
    Denver

79 Maps

83 Eating Olives in the House of Heartbroken Women

I

LETTERS TO EROS

Your body that includes everything
you have done, you have had done
to you and goes beyond it

This is not what I want
but I want this also.

   —Margaret Atwood

I had forgotten
the gods, now

in attendance as you
unlace, eyelet

by eyelet, this bodice
my body is

   —Marilyn Krysl

Finale for a Girl in a Skirt Sewn of Sky

You are distance. The night
woven into clothing. Planetary
and periwinkle-blue, the chalky
hue of galaxies.

You are point A and point B—
the space between clothespins
that line the wire like musical notes
holding up the melancholy of damp shirts.

You are space and particle.
The dust motes that float
around my face when I sweep the bedroom
free from last night's lasciviousness.

You are disease so intrusive
the bones in my wrist dissolve
to sand and are deposited on a beach
I've never been to.

You are this poem. Its inability to be
linear. The black nettings of letters.
You are its interstices, perched
between the misgivings of words.

You are this field I walk through. Both mist
and vista as my feet imprint the wet
grass before it springs back.
As if no bodies had ever been there.

Letters from a Lover from Another Planet

Here, we listen with our tongues, mouths always
open. When his tongue searches the damp
cellar of my throat, he recalls
stories I've forgotten, recites the name
of every lover that's ever kissed
the inside of my armpits. He knows
what I want and what I don't
like about the way he reads the history
of my hair as if each strand
were a declarative sentence.
He tells me I'm too eager to please.
You must learn to take, to say "give me"
graciously. He likes what's inside—
not soul, or metaphysical heart but the real
blood-chugging organ: its russet
muscularity; the way it blooms
bright as an anthurium beneath the white
trellis of ribs; its allegretto beat. *The sweeping*
of blood through ventricles is sexier
than breasts, he declares as he places his tongue
on my wrist, tells me to pay attention
to the vignettes of legs, the backsides
of knees, for each cell holds a story.
Open your mouth, he says. *Leak*
the letters of your name into my lungs,
the milkweed smell of your skeleton,
the bloodroot of you.

The Fix-it Man

I want a man who can fix things:
solder and suture the mechanical
entrails of appliances, redeem
beef stew from too much salt, sew
coat pockets so I don't lose
my wallet with a picture of him
rehanging the chandelier
that dropped like a meteor when I danced
lambada beneath it. I'm high
maintenance, a natural disaster—
light bulbs shatter when I pass, toilets
overflow, children next door
in bright white rooms dream
of car collisions, collapsing
buildings. I want a man
who can install a notch filter
at the end of a coaxial cable
for free access to the Playboy channel—
which we'll watch while he fixes me
Capellini de Mare, removes knots
from my cataclysmic hair, makes me come
with his fingers alone. A man with hands
the span of a plate, but fingers so skin-
sensitive they can shave my legs, the summits
of knees without a nick. Replace
strings on my Martin then play it like he's
dialing my number. Not a plumber
or a surgeon but a fix-it man
who repairs and installs at no extra fee.

Red Dress

Midmorning, mid-February, mid-blizzard,
I pick up photos from a summer wedding
in Colorado and the first picture is me
all sass and flash in a red dress.

But it is the final photos on the roll
that I'd forgotten, taken several months later
of my lover reclined across my bed
in a blue sharkskin suit next to my friend.

They are laughing as if they were in love,
if you look closely though you'll see the boy is smiling
at the girl behind the lens although his hand
is on another girl's knee which seems appropriate to me

since in the end it was my skin he said
he felt nothing when he touched as if nothing were a feeling
and yet emptiness is never abstract when the body
drags, doubles its weight in the blue static of absence.

It seems some joke under the tyranny of gods
that these photos be juxtaposed. (The girl in the red dress,
the boy in the blue suit). They look nothing alike
yet they fit together: she beaming; he beautiful
in his asymmetrical grace.

The girl looks so frivolous I want to slap her
though she'll know soon enough a red dress
will never save her from sadness that soaks the bones
and burnishes the body to phosphorous.

Dazed by sun and alcohol, clutching a glass of Cabernet
she looks like she could high kick her way to California
where at least absence owns the ocean and lovers
give back in pictures what they've taken in real life.

And who, when looking at these two, could ever guess
the red dress would become a wilted petal on the floor
in front of a locked door; and the boy's smile would slip
into history's index, his face turning away from the camera,

away from the girl behind the camera
as she continues to photograph
his back as he disappears into the blue
fugue of a day that never awakened.

As If

for Jacob

Are you a fatalist or a nihilist? you ask
as if it matters
as if the night hurtling past
will pause so we might take stock
of the glittering web the moon lays at our feet
each bead of water
on each sheath of grass
an oasis
a lagoon
for a file of ants winding through the darkness
thin as Ariadne's thread
as if this poem will get me to heaven
as if sadness will save anyone
a strand of as ifs
that run up the back of legs like seams
like veins that burst
into rain clouds
immobilizing us
as if it matters where we get to
when we get to this
as if we have anywhere to go anyway
trapped by snow and the bitten lip of discontent
yet you sit at the kitchen table
your hand cupped around flame
cheeks hollowed by the suck of fire into your cigarette
the sweet sting of nicotine
as if the world hinged on that one small flare
as if I could lick light from your skin
and offer my tongue as a torch.

Tom Waits, I Hate You—

the way your voice snags
my skin when I'm waltzing
through a coffee shop, for the thousand
crows caught in your throat,
how it rains
every time I play "Tom Traubert's Blues."
I hate you for every valentine you never sent.
Call me indigo, azure, cerulean; call me
every shade of blue for being born
two decades after you.

I hate you for every cornfield, filling
station, phone booth I've passed with my feet
on the dash, listening to you pluck
nightingales from a piano; writhing
as if it were my ribcage being played
beneath a moon that is no grapefruit,
but the bottom of a shot glass.

For every bad relationship, every dead pet,
and every car I've wrecked
into light posts trying to tune you out;
for all the lost radios, Walkmans
tossed over bridges—still the sound of you
rising from water like a prayer at midday,
or the ragged song of cicadas
tugging frogs out of watery homes.

For every lounge lizard, raindog, barfly
I've met; for every vinyl booth I've been pushed
into by a boy with a bad haircut;
for every man I've fucked
according to the angle of his chin
or the color of his coat.

Tom Waits, I hate you.

Well, the night is too dark
for dreaming; the barman bellows out
last call; and you've turned me into a gun-
street girl with a pistol and a grudge
and an alligator belt, a pocket
full of love letters
that have never been sent.

Inflorescence

It was spring, I was fourteen.
The ground stained with the juice
of mulberries, their plump bodies
pecked by blue jays and other air-born
scavengers. In the backseat
of a station wagon my date
fumbled with my bra, the hook
and clasp concept out of his grasp.
A football player, his blunt fingers were
accustomed to larger things. His mouth warm,
wet, tasting faintly of smuggled
cigarettes and the chalky
sweetness of apricots—the smell
of youth before the body
begins its backslide into decline.
Fine gold hair sprouted on my calves
like the silky pelts of corn. Unlike
the cheerleaders at school whose smooth legs
high-kicked, their red skirts
umbrellas over the yellow
suns of polyester underpants.
A collective sigh from the stadium: girls whose
bodies hadn't yet gained grace,
popularity; boys whose erections
pressed against the zippers of Wranglers, small
indentations of desire. That year
azaleas were so profuse
my mother placed a vase on each
sill of our house, shades ranging from the bright,
light pink of bubble gum
cheerleaders blew into blossoms—
their mouths more adept at bubbles,
at love—to the dark magenta of the janitor's

lips, a Spanish woman named Guadalupe:
Our Holy Mother she translated for me after class
as she pulled gum from beneath desks.
I drifted from Geology to Math,
only interested in the circumference
of an open mouth, the cylinders of limbs,
proof that I wasn't the only virgin in my class,
the word *virgin* delicate
as disease, my best friend already
slathered in honey and licked—
a thousand bees' wings fluttering against flesh;
proof that bodies fall together
as naturally as the weddings of roots
to soil, light to leaves.

The Problem with Celibacy

The body has its own idea of rebellion.
It leans into strangers, gas-station
attendants, the Piggly Wiggly
check-out boy; it presses itself against
the hot hoods of running cars.

Your body embarrasses you: the
architecture of its plush flesh, its need
for touch. You can't visit
the local bar without propositioning
the bartender, pressing your pelvis

against the bouncer as you stumble
out of nightclubs into the street
where lampposts illuminate couples
kissing, caressing, grinding
while trees whisper obscenities.

The shuffle of leaves on sidewalks rasp
like skin. The heat from asphalt rises
up your thighs in a tongue of hot air.
The cats in the alley are a constant
reminder of your status.

Even shadows are attractive. You stop
eating chocolate, kiwis, oysters for fear
of mauling the mailman. You lock
yourself in your house where you
rub against the fur of TV static.

You toss out your Turrentine albums, freesia-
scented soap, silk pajamas. Everything
is sex. Your radio goes, magazines, kitchen
towels. Until your house is bare,
sterile. You breathe easier

but then notice the body's natural
pulsations: heartbeat, eyeblink, breathing.
There is nothing that isn't a metaphor.
Outside, it is humid, the city smells
like breath, the madness of teeth.

So you throw open windows and doors,
air thick with calendula, heat,
the silver trill of crickets
sends you reeling into spring and
a renegotiation with desire.

Toledo Bend

Green apples,
crisp as organdy.
Tangle of lips,

an embrace:
blades of wet
grass, leaves

circling in a
whirlpool of wind,
a scattering of

grackles foraging
in a lake
iridescent with scales

of bluegill,
algae's lengthy fingers.
Burst of diamonds

flung from feathers
of a pelican
as it lifts

off the water.
Hibiscus and fish
seep through

the mesh
nets we sleep
on in sunlight,

beneath mimosa's firework
flowers, sanguine as
flame; a breath

in our blood,
a crocus opening
in our throats.

The Air Lost in Breathing

A woman imagines two bodies
coming together like a button
closing, unclosing two sides of a shirt:
a pattern of holes, a vacancy
strategically placed over her stomach.

Is it always the same? she wonders.
The same airless, treeless, windowless
space after a disappearance, a separation
of hands. She gestures to her mirror, her gold
signifier no longer flashing a response.

With her right hand she scripts
her lips into a kiss and pressing her mouth
to mine, she acknowledges two
people who can never
walk out on one another.

Denali Highway

Late summer, I think of you, during afternoon siestas
when the fan oscillates and the air
sifting through the blinds smells faintly of rain,
lemongrass and the scent of your skin after sleep:

your low voice—Johnny Cash imitations,
your penchant for Red Nuts and the way
the bones would lift out of your face
when you played for me, switching

from banjo to guitar with the ease of a man
who slid from one town to the next, one
woman to another. I remember fireweed,
the Alcan, my Texas T-shirt, the Totem Cafe,
coffee and coffee and coffee
and playing tic-tac-toe on the frosted

windshield of your pick-up. We would sleep
in the Westfalia as it rained, the flicker
of leaves against the window as our bodies
curved against one another. I still sleep
with my knees curled into my stomach,

wonder what happened to you. The last time
I saw you, you stood in the middle
of Denali highway, yelling at me through the rain.
I recall the sound of syllables,
water-ruined and muffled, but still
the wet trill of your mouth—opening,
closing on my name.

His Black Scrawl

spiderwebs my heart. *The river of ignorance*
covers most of my regrets, he writes
on a postcard from Alaska. On the
reverse, lupine and fireweed
line Denali highway like patriotic
streamers. In the background, the snow-
glazed tundra reminds me of the wilderness,
this wildness now gone from me
like him, who remains running
a fishing boat outside Talkeetna. He writes
of the bush, silver salmon and cracked
geodes with amethyst. He says
I want too much and he is farther from me
than the bottom of the Pacific and,
of course, I like him more for it.
In my backyard, persimmons are bloated
with beetles and the figs have fallen
to the ground as summer dissolves and I
want to reply but the landscape
lies between us like a callused hand,
hard to the touch, unwilling to hold.

The Body's Migration

"When I say body what is that a word for?"
                                        —Margaret Atwood

Is it these arms, pale as sun-bleached pebbles, the blue
creeks of arteries? These lips, soft as moth
wings and drawn to conflagrations

as well? Or this belly
plump with water, the roots of calla lilies
blooming in the womb?

Perhaps not parts, but whole: the body
as cross, as snow angel—spread-eagled
for flight but pinned to the ground

by disease that settles
light as dust, then gains the weight
of granite; or is it the body's movement

as it trudges from birth to midlife crisis
to finale of body, the end
of skin—first a husk

like a sheet with no bodies
beneath it, then a breath, a melody,
a dirge. This body that migrates to your body,

its idiosyncrasies of skin: moles
that spread across the vista of back
like desiccant desert plants, scars

from barbed wire, the cicatrix
beneath the chin
from continuous childhood tumblings.

This body that finds your body in the dark
by its hooded light, the curve of mandible
and knee, the elbow's angular grace.

The belly button, dark star, black hole to an
ocean where your skin sheds light like the white
flesh of pears and rain gathers on eyelids, the nimbus

of your face as you say my name with the delicacy
of a monarch that's taken refuge in the moist,
warm grotto of your infinite mouth.

Open Letter to Eros

I want a love that is imprecise, one
that sprawls over the bed, spills out windows,
disrupting churchgoers as they stroll
across the green glow of mowed lawns. I want
a love that commandeers the world, a bone-
clanking, hydrant-splashing, dog-
salivating affair. The ravaged and
the ravenous—those lycanthropes of lust.

No candy hearts or delicacies
of language. Do not ask me
to be demure, clean or to go
with the flow. I am electric.
I sprinkle poison
in the bird feeder, watch blue jays
fall like insatiable kisses.

I want fuck and prick
and cunt. Those delicious monosyllables
of want. I want you in a chair
handcuffed and desiring me so badly
even your feet are on fire. I want
love that is black as a highway
on a starless night, black as madness, sable
smooth and impenetrable. I want love
to write a love poem to me
with bad intentions.

Love is my nemesis,
my neurosurgeon, the unruly
child, the car that won't steer
straight, the boy on a skateboard
carving the street
into attraction and repulsion.

I want a love that is contradictory, indelible
and edible, a love that relishes
imperfections and requisitions the moon.
A love that isn't afraid of grief, sadness,
the small crimes we commit
against ourselves; love as cool
as a bruise, sensitive as skin
on eyelids, nipples and ears.

I want a love that listens:
to rain a half mile
before it hits the house; to the feather
brushing sound of morning glories as they close
their petals for rain's arrival; the soft
shuffle of beetles as they begin a slow
crawl across the orchard into the sweet
red bellies of fallen apples.

II

WHEN WE BREATHE

It is the shape beneath the shape
that summons us.

—Charles Wright

Branches

You still won't let me touch that part of you
where your upper arm is welded to your side
in a mass of melted tissue, but you allow me
the welts on your back, that I take
in my hands when the moon
shadows your skin with hills,
gullies and I spend hours rubbing as if I could
smooth the lines away, smooth

the mirror of your father from your face.
It remains in the broken
curve of your nose, your hazel eyes, and the color
of your back, the same pale as my palm: *a body
should have scars*, your father said as he criss-
crossed your back with his belt,
branches, steel wire. A *back
should look like a hand*, and he carved
grooves into you as if you were wood
or wax. Your back of bone,
your back like a tree circled by lightning,
the scent of evergreen and sweat
filling the thin ravine where your spine
pulls the two sides together like wings
and my fingers spread against your nape.

As I listen for the soft hiss of sleep,
the fine hair on your neck rises
then settles at my caress. A *body
should burn*, your father said as he poured
gasoline on you while you slept, your small
figure curled into a fist. What more
to say? Your back, my hand—that reads
this parchment of scars connecting us
in a calligraphy of grief and delicate flesh.

Insomnia

It is true. We do carry the dead
in the soles of our feet. Each
morning I do the widow's

walk. My heels are swelling
with Christmas cards from dead
relatives, a hair clip that flew

from grandmother's head when she
crashed through the windshield.
Heaven is in the body, they
write, *and we like yours.*

When I crumble into bed,
Uncle Buddy cracks black
walnuts in my left knee, Aunt Nan
splits kindling in my ankles.

They splinter my legs
into wood chips, build
bonfires, my flesh flushed
with an unidentifiable rash.

I cried when Uncle Seamus
hooked himself on a barb
wire fence, died of gangrene,

now I spend my nights cursing
his snores, hawks, coughs and off-
key singing that rack my body.

I want my calves back, free of card
tables, peppermint schnapps,
eyes ogling me as I masturbate.

No more whining in my head
when it presses itself to the pillow;
I want silence and sleep and to only

think of you when it suits my mood
to play post office for the dead.

The Jesus Apostrophes

I.

Jesus, I enter you as fool's gold
pan-flashing in the pit
of your hungry stomach.
I enter you, a trail of cable
looping through your dove-colored bones.
I enter you like whippoorwills
foretelling death, like the benedictions
of a banjo's silver sting.
Listen Jesus, my love,
I'm no saint, I'm red-hot,
heart-shaped candy: all sweetness
and no sustenance.
I enter you like the lubriciousness
of molasses, humidity's glue, the corn-syrup
thickness of two bodies rattling their bones
on a deck overlooking the Pacific.
Bite my arm and your teeth
fall away in stars. Your mouth
a dark lake where I was baptized
but never saved.

II.

I spasmed at my baptism
when the the preacher tilted me
back into the Mulberry River. He said
he felt God pass through me.
I didn't tell him
it was the cold blow of water
on my skull and the loneliness
of his large hands

smelling of turpentine, the chemical
lemon scent of furniture polish.
And how could I ever be saved,
when at that moment, instead of envisioning Baby Jesus,
all I could see was the preacher on his knees
dusting each pew as he hummed "Amazing Grace"
with an ache in the vacuum of his voice
that made the stained-glass windows shake
as he looked up for a crack
in the sky, a fissure
he could climb through, hanging
on the rim of Heaven,
where God hovers, before lifting
His Almighty two-ton, steel-toe boot
to grind the preacher's bleeding,
citrus-scented fingers.

III.

It's midnight, Christmas Eve. My relatives attend
service at Mansfield Baptist with boys
I used to kiss in pick-up trucks: now men, married
and moral, reading Ecclesiastes about the unwise,
wicked ways of women.

I like wicked women, my newly married friend,
Brian, announces as we speed in my cousin's
convertible to Clear Lake where clay
flames in headlights on the bankside
above the honey thickness of swamps.

As my relatives kneel, light candles in church,
my cousin and I, Brian and his wife, drag
on cigarettes sweet as hymns and offer up prayer
to our own blurred gods. Counting Crows'
"Long December" blares

on the only static-free station. In the dark
lacuna of this parked car, music is salvation
as Brian slips his hand between my thighs
while kissing and muttering love
nothings to his wife, who's too stoned to notice.

Farther down the road, boys frog-gig.
Beam of flashlights flicker
through the moss of Cypress trees.
Their yelps ring across the lake
like a succession of skimmed stones

as I brush Brian's hand away, focus
on the wafer light
of winter stars, barely
visible through the black
scratchings of barren branches.

Girls Gathered for a High School Photo, Circa 1960

Girls with arms like rivers highlighted by skylight, sighs
soft as cattails. Girls with lips so smooth

you could slide off the side of the world, discover
nothing beneath your feet but evening and Saturn's smoky rings.

Girls like lampposts, eyes the color of asphalt glittering
in the distance, scent of rain rising from their wrists.

Girls with smiles like knives cutting wedding-cake,
their cheeks the color of conch shells, pale faces

calm as a pond, underneath rock and weed.
Girls like my mother, her voice, yellow petals

floating above a thorny branch.

Your Limbs Are Knotted Ropes

You look like a concentration camp victim.
You are the most beautiful person I've seen.
Delicate, sharp as the icicle
hanging like a huge translucent tooth
from the eaves of my back porch.
The bones of your knees, hips
jut out in sharp stones. Skin
slides over them like water. You are
my *cordilla*. My eyes scale the rungs
of your bones. You notice me
noticing you, you think
it's because you have cancer.
It is. You swing on the hinge
of the world. Each gesture
pointed. I want to hold your edges,
dance tooth to tooth, limb
to knotted limb. Climb into you. Ascend
into the mouth of your survival.

Blackberries

Sundays, after sermons at Benson Baptist,
my mother and I would go blackberry picking.
Shredding our fingertips; our hands
purpled with berry stain
and blood. In that fortress of thorns
we discovered a fox skull and black-
eyed Susans, blooming like miniature suns
through the dark thicket of green. Each

of our findings was momentous: the flowers
plucked and put in a vase; the fox skull
polished and placed in the window
as a sentinel of sleep. And always, my mother
with a bruised face, but fingers
tenacious as roots, offering
berries that throbbed like cuts
when we closed our mouths around them.

Love Travels in the Pockets of Old Men

On the histories of tongues
love's detritus lies
saliva-imbued and burdensome
like the words of childhood
veranda   egret   jacaranda
we stumbled and stuttered our way through
and now twenty years later,
choking on love's
staccato song
                I want
                        I don't want
that clacks against teeth
like a congregation of preachers.

It is Sunday and all day I have paced
my kitchen trying to figure out
love's configuration—
but the heart
remains incomputable.
                Listen Love,
                     I'm through
with your incessant clanging; the bell tolls
in the late afternoon, color of whey,
the rooftops of houses grey and slaked
with rain. A blue light flares
in the steeple of a church as an
old man strolls the street
his face creased, pale as a page
from the Bible. He looks up
into rain; love is what travels
in his pocket as he walks home alone
to his veranda where jacaranda bloom
and egrets eat their blossoms.

Le roi

a girl repeats to the rain
a name that's silk and syllables
elongated on the tongue—silt
     sliding into the river.

Pineapple pears, peridot bulbs,
break from the branch
with the weight of rain and maturation,
a dull thud as they collect
in pools of mud like a fist
hitting the soft delta of stomach.
      Every act of nature
acquires a human narrative.
Like biting into bruised fruit
it is what we want
and what we don't want
      that keeps us dragging our knuckles
on the bedside, taking inventory
of faces that flash like lanterns in a long,
dark corridor. Recognition
      accumulates with the delicacy of frost.
We can't help ourselves—this need
for metaphor, or more simply, metaphor's
desire for collision.
    I want to kiss you.
I apologize for my want.
I would prefer to pass it down the medieval table,
pawn it, trade it for a pair
of velvet boots,
    a picture of a courtyard
where a girl dreams of the emperor
of rain; pears heavy
as breasts in his fluid palms; the pale

arc of the pelvis
              as it crests into waves.

In the yard, the girl gathers the bruised fruit
in the bowl of her shirt while a man
lingers behind a screen door. Plaster
falls within the wall.
                          The proteus is in furious
bloom,
          spilling like billets-doux across the lawn.

Pears keep falling
              rain keeps falling
The man presses his lips
to the mesh screen where rust spreads like breath,
dust of all things left untouched.

Sin

is a Southern composition.
Something about the way the day
slides open like sorghum:

ooze and illusion of slowness.
We're all trailer trash
alcoholics or debutantes:

skin thin as tulle.
But when we gather at the levee
we're song and drizzle,

the elongation of a grey-
drenched day. Scattering of
fireflies pinpoint

our failures and revivals
in the name of god
even when god's disappeared

in the river, after taking
our breath; placing a levy
on our stuttering hearts.

When We Breathe

Our breath is the color of absence,
sleet, the frozen pond behind a house
where catfish and water moccasins weave in
and out of the watery door of melting ice
like strands of hair, the delicate
husks of dead loves.

Clouds shift across the sky
in broken ice floes; sleet filters
through the silver pores of a screen door
with a wide gap where the wire frays—
a baseball thrown off course by a young boy
with wavy hair and a lopsided smile.

These are the entrances, exits
of our everyday lives where the boy
drowns, his forehead tapping against ice, while
a woman with white hair, unaware, chops
onions and a man lingers behind her, humming
a song that's never had words.

Loneliness

I asked Hank Williams "How lonely does it get?"
Hank Williams hasn't answered yet.
                    —Leonard Cohen

It's small. Multiple. It collects
on windows like rain
or rice thrown on the floor of a church
after a wedding. Tears flung
in a confession booth. It scatters.

Hank reclines on the divan, smoking
a cigarillo, trying to recall the name of the song
playing when we first met. It
scratches at the door. The smell
of fever drifts through the room
and the remembrance of rain, so fine
it felt of hair, a thousand blue kisses.
I love the way your hair smells, Hank tells me,
his breath cold sleet, fingers pale
as ghost fishes brush across my breasts.

It's a lesson in forearms,
the sinew and ache of embrace. A tightening
in the air before a storm, when spoons
rattle in drawers, and the faucet
leaks like a metronome. It deludes

and denudes us. I tell my mother
I'm in love with a ghost.
How tragic, she replies as Hank
serenades me from the bathroom.
You know I don't cook, I remind him.

It's a soliloquy to trees,
a whole night of touch, then the aftermath

of nothing; a season of forgetting, of listening
to the steadfast weeping of a neighbor
through the heat grill.
It's a punctured vein, a disruption
of blood, a lament for the body
bivouacked on a bed of seashells.

Let's get sushi, Hank says and at the restaurant
the waitress pours saki while the windows shake
with hail. She serves loneliness
on a platter wrapped in seaweed and cold
as Hank's breath, but able to be eaten.

It's a legacy, says Hank
as our feet float off without us,
two ghosts, reduced to a refrain
about heartache, tears and departures.
Outside, loneliness gathers in the throats of dogs
while sleet cripples corn stalks and wind
rummages the empty pockets of an apron
clipped to a wire.

Refrains in Elkins, Arkansas

Solitude is a German Ruger, my mother
would say and through the thin walls
of our bedrooms I could hear the refrain
of the gun chamber clicking. Those nights,
I'd tiptoe to the back porch where clouds
churned into witches and rain
trailed off the black shadows of trees.

The darkness was punctuated with a bullfrog's
rumble and the distant trill of crickets.
Jags of lightning forced my eyes shut:
like my left eye, closed and swollen for a week
from the punch Walter Sledge threw me
on the school bus. The redbuds
and dogwoods in bloom, that was the year

our neighbors asked us to go to auctions, crawfish
boils and bluegrass. We never went, though
sometimes we heard the invitations
of fiddles: *Come and sit by my side, say you love me,*
do not hasten to bid me adieu. . . The trembling
strings of our discontent reverberated
through the firefly-laden forest as my mother

pulled me in. *Go to sleep,*
she'd say, *and dream of things that fly,*
while the cloud witches whispered
through the sleet-glazed window panes
as the steel chamber of the Ruger
turned the phrase into a dissonant hymn.

Negative

I can still hear grey
tinted windows breaking
like dominoes clicking together,

your shoulders framed
by the windshield and the glass
spraying out like miniature

stars on the black macadam.
In this darkness of pupils,
bones, the night is tedious

in its absence of color.
The spiderweb light
of constellations is not

bright enough to keep me
from dreaming of you,
as I hold

my own hand and awake
to the taste of anise, chewing
my tongue as if it were licorice

behind the headlights of teeth.
My mouth overflows
with the sun's red glare.

It Is the Cloud-Shingled Sky that Sends Me Back to You

On a morning when the sun isn't shining
and the street is coated with the oily
blood of a deer, I think of you when we stood
your chest to my back and you
pulled me into you like water
into a glass. *Water*
is love, is luck, you used to say.

You, with crevices etched into your skin
like a blueprint of a battle
that never occurred, whose face
spoke of wars, weddings: two acts
you did not believe in. In your pocket,
zinc pennies, Alexander Pope and *Le Monde*
rubbed restlessly against a hipbone
conceived of music.

When you died, the mortician discovered words
he'd never heard spill from your body
in the space of siphoned blood, while I
said your name over and over
until it became a chant; and focused
on the odor of magnolia fuscata
filtering through the screen, palmettos
swollen with rain, elephant grass
breaking with the weight of water.

Bone-flower

Somewhere the moon sifts through a crack
in a wall, somewhere there is a light
that isn't turned on, somewhere
a woman sleeps in the dark
of a windowless room while the night
avalanches and in the white silence
of her sleep, a seven-year-old
hangs from the magnolia in the backyard:
his face bloodless, bone-flower,
a pendulum of legs that swing
back and forth like the tick
of a grandfather clock—a present
shipped from Italy, abandoned

in a room the color of bone, the woman
spins before a red door, a wide
wound that opens into her father's bedroom.
The walls bare except for the grandfather
clock that locates her heart, a picture
of a young boy. Through a crack
in the wall she peers at the frame of a lake,
grey with rain, a shifting magnolia;
the click of a lock
straightens her spine and the photo on the wall
trembles. Her father's room
is a box, a dungeon, and the clock

is a passage outside where
the lake searches for the white
grimace of moon, like the smile on her father's face
when he unlocks the door to bring her hearts
of palm, blood oranges, the suffocating
fingers of his love. Sleet

nets the windowpanes while the lake
swallows the moon, her father
swallows her hands and there is no lamp,
no door, no heartbeat—only
a ravening wind in a windowless room.

On Hearing My Father Pulled a Shotgun on My Grandparents during Thanksgiving Dinner

All my relatives seated: Louellyn and her new husband,
Aunt Nan and Laura May, Uncle Buddy passing
mashed potatoes, toasting God, good food, and the lack
of family deaths this year. Everyone flying, driving home
for that day when families convene and I laugh,
imagining my father strolling in, ·
uninvited, shotgun on hip, his red hair
tangled and cow-licked, beer-gut
protruding from the hem of his T-shirt, shooting
the turkey and everyone splattered
not with blood, but celery,
oyster stuffing, droplets of grease.

I have always held my father up
in one hand, everyone else in the other
as if on a set of scales
and my grandparents, my mother and I
sink while my father floats there
weightless and grinning. I refused to see
my father's grief: a wife who divorced him, a daughter
who hates him, his liver dissolved, his angular
cheeks now pockets of flesh, veined
and sallow. I only saw
how the nights he didn't come home
were a relief to us all. But for once, alone,
a thousand miles from the South and not
part of the argument, I think about my father
as a boy, rising at 4:30 to milk cows
before school, an ache in his stomach
from too little sleep and on days when he was too sick

to get out of bed, his father, my grandfather,
would jerk him up, belt in hand, and he
would trudge to the dairy with the crack
of a belt echoing in his ears.

A young boy with hair
shooting out in bright-red spirals, his body
wiry, pale as cream, perched
on a stool, waiting for the sun as his body
shook with anger, the sting of leather, the chill
of a southern dawn and the only heat
came from the cow's moist noisy breath
as he squeezed her udders for milk, formed
clouds with his mouth in the dissipating dark.

Eating Honeybuns on the Louisiana Highway

It's been two decades since I was in this Southern
land regaining my drawl. The highway
crumbles away; the only grocery
between Converse and Mansfield
perches on the side of the road like
a broken-down Buick; each year
one of my grandmother's mutts is shot
in the heart by quail hunters; the catfish pond,
where my grandfather and I fished, exists,
choked with leaves, pine needles and algae.

The house is still dark paneling
with a yellow kitchen but the ceiling is lower,
the shelves I couldn't quite get to are
in reach. My grandfather is shorter
than I am. His legs, which carried
the sturdiness of a farm,
are only slightly larger than my arms.
His emphysema's so bad he needs
a machine to breathe—still
he smokes. It's too late for plea-
bargains, threats, so I pull up a chair,
slug a beer with him, take a few
drags of his Merit.

If only death could be this
watching hummingbirds hover
at the feeder; or eating honeybuns
on the Louisiana highway as we drive
to the pond before the sun rises,
to watch herons skim the unlit
ripples of this black water.

Undone

It was your thin reticulate skin
that drew me near, the way your tongue
scissored and whispered, *Eat, girl. Eat.*

You said my teeth glowed like peonies
in a rainstorm and I was too impressed
to do anything but lie down in the orchard,

a litany of saints rattling in my throat. I am a woman
punctuated by quotation marks. It was the coil
and the choreography of you moving through the tree

like a lesson in song. Daybreak, and morning
falls out from under me. The learning of words
begins: *xanthic, ichor, egress. . .*

Egrets float above us like scraps of fabric.
My dress evaporates: what's left
is a ribbon of emeralds and venom.

       *   *   *

Did you smear your skin with jasmine
and cop to God? Did you bring
good news from the garden,
or are you startled by the dark
yard of yearning before you?
You've been here before. You were born
to believe in treachery.

       *   *   *

Our bodies our sieves: through the ear
passes a song, out comes a war.
I spit the histories of women in corsets
eating quince in hammocks

overlooking the gullies of myths.
Don't say you've never dreamed of me.
I am that thread you feel at the back of your throat
I am that note you rise to when you come
I am the arc of your foot and the leverage of your thumb
I am the bone's marrow and sorrow, the elegance of neck,
the deathnote to your footnote,
the flesh whittled to one word.

III

EXHALATIONS

Don't you know *yet*? Fling the emptiness out of your arms
into the spaces we breathe; perhaps the birds
will feel the expanded air with more passionate flying.

—Rilke

Desire Takes a Road Trip to New Orleans

Desire changes her name to Desiree
so people will stop asking if she's an abstraction
or a reality. She buys a blue Nova, spins towards New Orleans
via Texarkana where she saunters into Ricky Dell's Roadhouse
for a Gibson chilled with onions that she pops
into her mouth before leaning over the bar
to lick the bartender. Eight days later,
he still shakes with the wisteria scent of her hair
and the sweet acid of onions hovering over his upper lip
where his mustache singed away.

All the matches in the bar are black by the time
Desiree shifts into second with the ease of a boy
switching his affections from his mother
to his first girlfriend that he finger-fucked in his Dad's
silver Impala beneath a moon hung in the sky
like a wind chime. The stars sounding out a song
that only those with an ocean beneath their ribs can hear.

At Trenton Episcopal, Desiree decides to use the bathroom.
The choir boys are singing *Hallelujah*
when she jaunts in like a lucky horseshoe. Suddenly,
their platelets ring her name while God's golden mallet
hammers away at their malleable, sin-soaked hearts.

When Desiree arrives on the esplanades, all the boys
on the bayou gather to sing, *with crooked hearts*
and crooked feet we flee, down a crooked road
as we pray, Oh Desiree. She slits her skirt
up her creole thigh, strides likes she's late for a date
with Dante Alighieri. She's got nowhere to go
but she likes the leg's elongation, the stretch
and flex of muscle, the way the calf
bunches up like a ball that she could spiderweb

the windows of those indifferent to her siren serenade.
And she knows if she practices her fastball
she'll shatter the glass ceiling of heaven and shards
will scatter the earth in a simulacrum of lust
as the flushed lips of sordid saints say,
Oh Desiree, Desiree, only to you we pray.

Desire's Exhalations and the Incidentals of Happiness

On a Line by William Carpenter

"The thief puts her behind the wheel and says *drive, baby*"
and she does, even though she's a southern belle—taught
men drive; women ride—she's happy
to hike up her tulle and taffeta skirt, frothy
as champagne's evaporating head, and zoom
out of the driveway, quick as desire, a dragonfly's
silver trajectory. She's ready to step up
and out, swap her satin pumps for a pair
of steel toes, kick the shit out of the next
sign that says: *Buckle Up. It's the Law.*

Right now, while the girl rips her debutante dress
on the gear stick, couples skinny dip
at her coming out party. In the aquamarine light
of her parent's pool, bodies gleam like bits
of glass; lingerie hung across lawn chairs in wilted petals, white
markers of surrender. The thief and the belle accelerate
for California, shifting through the darkness, over asphalt's glitter,
listening to the oldies' station: *Raindrops keep falling on my head*
floats in the distance between them and the thief hums;
You must be getting old, the girls says as the thief taps his cigarette
on the window, searching for silos, windmills—something
steady and Midwestern but the stars are like points
of icicles, and illuminate nothing.

The girl gets dizzy with the thickness of this night so they pull
      over
somewhere in Iowa to a dive bar called Rosa's.
The girl asks the thief to buy her a drink since her purse
is in his pocket. She is tired of her sweet tea

and lemonade life—she wants to imbibe a fire
hazard and there's a cute boy shooting pool that's checking
her out. While the girl tilts her head for a shot
of SoCo, sweet as a George Jones song, and country
swings with a boy whose belt buckle reads, *Bullseye,*
beneath the mute monitor of bombings in some foreign land,
the thief pees, writing the letters of his name in the cistern.
He used to be a car salesman before becoming a collector of maps,
Camel coupons, bras from famous porn stars.

He is living his life as he wanted
when he was seventeen. Now he wishes he could dance
naked across a golf course, not worry about
his developing paunch. He knows this life is not a walk-over,
it's a get-down, gotta-go shake and he's just now learning the
   rhythm
of roads, but the road he's on is an avenue called California
somewhere in Iowa where Traci Lords supposedly rented an
   apartment
with a three-car garage. *Drive, baby,* she says.
Into the static and pitch, past clotheslines,
combines, down the spine of Iowa's unravelling night.

Walking

"It so happens that I am tired of being a man."
—Neruda

It so happens that I am tired of being a woman
walking down sleet-glazed streets to the whistle
of tires and the guttural voices of men
puffing vanilla cigars in black Buicks.

It so happens that I am tired of my ponderous
breasts, my ponderous heart,
my calves, unsteady, unstable,
unable to hold up my upper half.

I sift into cafes, clouded with steam, clove smoke,
into second hand stores that sell velvet
bell-bottoms, belt-buckle shoes still wearing the odor
of their dead owners. Out into streets

where the grey mist of pollution sprawls
like a dingy tablecloth and the city offers her wares:
panhandlers with burnt bodies and limbs
lost to the Korean War or the bite of a Brown Recluse.

I do not want to be a window on an avenue
reflecting the gnarled calves of cancer-
ridden men and women scuttling
home to sitcoms, meatloaf, prayers.

I walk with my face and my hair
wet as my feet
lug behind me, trip over street
grills, oleander bushes while white

mannequins, lining store fronts,
gaze out upon the wet streets, hard

plaster arms trailing their unscarred
bodies like flightless wings.

Bell Peppers

I.

Most people think about it. The man fingering
yellow squash in Aisle One would
shove his shotgun in his mouth, the one he kills
quails with, suck the bullet right through his head.
The woman hiding in a velvet fedora imagines
accelerating to 80, 90, 130, over the Golden Gate, sunlight
splintering off her blue Subaru as it spins
through the air in a stream of tinsel.
The three-year-old crying by the potatoes thinks
of pedaling his tricycle in front of the mail truck. Even
the boy at the checkout counter tells the girl
at the Express Lane he wants to die by inferno.
I prefer Draino, she says. Then asks,
Paper or plastic?

II.

Between bins of papayas, navel
oranges, I search a woman
who clutches a child to her left hip, her hands
pausing over red bell peppers.
Her baby has no eyes, only small
pockets of scar tissue. She murmurs a song
by Jackson Browne. How does she get
up each morning, brew coffee, cut
corners off toast, while the baby
without eyes, cries in the high chair? She knows
her child will never see elephants, sequoias, a fish-
shaped birthday cake. She places the bell pepper
to her baby's face, skims it across her nose.
I hear the woman crying at 2:00 a.m. as she

69

leans over the crib, while the moon,
hovering in the darkness in a blister of light,
illuminates her baby's curled form. *Jamaica*,
she calls her. *Jamaica*. She envisions open
spaces, sand dollars, and a sun so bright
you have to close your eyes. The woman
humming, grasps a red bell pepper,
the size of a human heart, a boxer's fist
racking the thin wall of body.

The Etiquette of Shells

*I attend a jazz festival where I'll be faced with deciding what
to do with the shells from the unshelled peanuts I buy. Last
year I ate them standing by a trash can. However, standing
by a trash can in the hot sun is not something to which I look
forward. What to do?* —Concerned
                                        —*Chicago Tribune*, May '97

Is your house immaculate? The wicks
of candles still white? Do you perch,
scarecrow woman, on a cream couch, savoring
the full moons of a sliced banana
with a fork, the skin already a yellow
blur down the steel throat of the disposal?

Friend, it is too easy to make fun of you,
for haven't we all asked the same inane
questions?—filling the starve of days
with trivia, imagining we corner
the market on immortality, our bodies
fragile as a foreseeable car wreck.

It isn't the question so much as the time you spent
to pen it, send it, then await a reply as if receiving
a letter from a relative in some Pakistani
prison. Even Miss Manners is exasperated,
asking: *Do I have to think of everything?*
Her advice is to carry a bag; I say, dance on a table

so hard your heels spark. Let shells
accumulate at feet like accolades. Leave
a trail. Merengue with a man
who doesn't speak your language.
Live messy.

Arizona

There is a woman in the street
shouting and shaking her hands
at some face in the sky
that is invisible to passersby; I say,
I know how you feel. She pauses,
falls out of her private patois
to ask me if I'm English. *No,
but I spent time in Australia. Ahh,
kangaroos,* she acknowledges; then dismisses
me to return to her argument with the sky.
She resides two blocks from me;
I have designated her
Arizona for the brand of iced
tea she asks me to buy
pressing two dollars in food stamps
into my hand because the Circle K
eighty-sixed her. I return with tea
and change and she asks me if I think
she resembles a spider; then, she is off
again, muttering in tongues,
her fingers moving back
and forth across her forehead
as if she were unravelling her face.
Perhaps, she is insane
or else something was set loose
inside her like the flapping
of wings in rain, the way windows
shake during a storm: a dull
rattling, then an implosion of glass.

There Is a Word for It

There is a word for it somewhere,
I'm sure. Maybe over there where the river
folds stones into silk smooth pebbles, or in the air
above the copperhead where dogwoods and redbuds
lace their petals together like fingers.

Maybe it is in the ivy-invaded pavilion
where the rain makes small rivers
for blue-backed lizards to swim in. Or in
the greenhouse where my calico cat
hides behind golden-edged elephant ears.

And could it be in the garden
between columns of corn
where the moon turns stalks
into a band of knights?—
a frieze of silver-tipped swords.

There is a word for it. Right
here in my bedroom
in the Ozarks where the rain
unfurls against French windows and lightning
illuminates a deer peering in.

Night-Blooming Cereus

In the morning
                    bijoux-bright
our imperfections evident
in the scrutiny of light—fantail
of stretch marks on hips, a brown mole
below the left knee like a lone survivor
of a battle—it's not going anywhere.
Breasts full and rounded when I stand
fall to the side as I lie. Light's
companion—the eye
is a supervisor
                    critical as cancer
beneath its unwavering gaze
we fumble in skin,
graceless as laundry
flapping on the line.

But when the sun goes down and the lamp's
turned off we're all fur, plush
flesh and scent of sandalwood.

Let the jet sluice of night
deceive us, let our limbs
unfold with the languor of rain;
                              frost collects like small stars
on the spines of cacti as we lie
slack-jawed and serene in slumber's
                              unlit bungalow.

It is in this field,

not a metaphor for soul or
bursting with gold
sunflowers, that the grass
is ochre and crunches
like small bones
of sparrows in the pink
plush mouth of a cat.

It is in this field
bordered by a broken
fence and Sweet William,
where memory and recitation
merge with the half-
lives of love.

In the eastern corner
a tractor that hasn't moved
since 1978 rusts
in the sleet of a Southern
winter.

This expanse of land
where nine years became ten,
then twenty-one; even now I can't
keep from wandering the edges,
plucking up black-eyed Susans.

While this field is not the soul
and the soul not
something I believe in—
there are voices here
that are more than tremolos
of breeze and grass.

It is the sound of memory

recalling itself. It is the sound
of my voice, my grandfather's voice
calling in the Hereford.
It is the voice of years passing
and gathering
like this batch of black-eyed Susans,
sturdy, wild, yellow bracts, roots
dangling but attached.

Reading Ed Ochester on the Plane from Chicago to Denver

The sun explodes in the sky
in a melodrama of orange and magenta
light that wavers like liquid on the horizon.
To my left, the wing shakes—a white flag
signaling surrender. Below, altocumulus clouds
riffle like whitecaps of waves or the padded
satin of a coffin. (I can't fly
without thinking about dying.)
 44 degrees in Denver, partly cloudy
the pilot announces as the seat belt signal beeps off.
I remain stationary. The kid next to me
performs sign language out the window
at some extraterrestrial ship while I read Ed Ochester
who writes a poem about Dr. Spock
and dying and I think about Rick,
the married chef in Colorado
who called me in Chicago to ask me out,
and dying.
 I'm also thinking about my high school
reunion and how I wish I had a dress
resplendent as a sunset and that Rick
wasn't married so I could get a little action
which never happens in Chicago
because I don't wear enough black
and my wisdom teeth are coming in.
Men can sense the agony of my mouth
and avoid it
 the way people stay away from funerals
if they can help it. Ed would come to my funeral though.
He'd bring his cats, a sprig of mint. Maybe chrysanthemums,
the color of explosions, and a poem about sunsets,

death, and the importance of mint
for a mouth exploding with teeth
and the need to be kissed
by a man not already married, not a high school
sweetheart either, or death's fetid lips. . .
        Ed might say I'm experiencing the exponential factor
of nostalgia. I'd just say, *kiss me,*
I got the signal.

Maps

I.

Sprawled in your blue bedroom, door
ajar—the orange walls of your den
flare like some exotic fruit: Gauguin's
Woman With Mango—her blue dress
a backdrop for the juice
sluicing down her neck, pooling
in the collarbone's lagoons.
Desire manifests itself in the fissures
of lips, the pads of fingertips.
Gauguin knew this, transferring Tahiti's
lust and lush to canvas.
Tahiti, so many miles away
yet the sea is here in my ear.

I don't know if when I wake
this room will be an illusion and you
a handmade postcard sent to the wrong address, someone
already calling to reclaim you.
But when you look up Shreveport, Louisiana
on the map, it is easy to be charmed.
A boy searching for a red dot that marks
the origins of this girl as he navigates
her flesh with his tongue: this cartography
that begins with skin
and moves her to a country she's never been to

where the ocean is a postdiluvian blue wound.
In the interval between mango-gold sky
and indigo—the quick collapse of day
into night as the Pleiades
loosen their light and sand dollars

spark like stars—she can no longer tell if the sky
lies above or below,
but with each step her burnt feet
heal as they tread the misty
lip of sea; its waves
bone chip and recompense.

II.

We fall in love. We fail
with the regularity of rain
in April. Lose friends to suicides, bad
habits, crashes. Worry about the surge
of traffic at five as we search
the blueprint of face for new
furrows. We forget
the forest at the fringe of city,
hunkering down at night
in the wells of beds.
Mornings we rise, spread
orange marmalade on a baguette;
our reflection in the toaster
startles us.

In this slipstream
of routine, the swell and expel
of each day, he comes to her
like a fever, reflecting light in the grey
stasis of morning. He comes
with the languor of rain. He comes
to her like a car wreck—incendiary
and sad. He comes with crumbs
on his tongue, a smear of marmalade
on his collar. He comes to her
bearing an atlas, a melody and tattoos

as she reinvents the world
in the compass of his wind-struck face.

III.

She calibrates her heart
as if it were a Swiss watch
yet this ringing in her body
will not stop: church bells and train whistles,
sirens and bicycle chimes. The phone
jangling from a foreign country: hello, allo, ahoy
a boy calls from the barge across the bay
beneath the calculus of galaxies. His voice,
a carillon pealing in her blood, its bright
pitch fantailing through her body like yellow
silk scarves and though the dark sea
yawns in the distance she is so light her eyes
flare like phosphor, her hips
flashing like hubcaps on the dirt road
of this country that isn't on any map.

IV.

During sex, he notices she's shy.
How can she tell him most evenings
she slumbers with her hands
tucked neatly between her legs

like a bookmark; when he opens her thighs
she's afraid they'll spill
histories that have inhabited her flesh for so long
they might start breathing

without her. Her pale legs are like pages
of an atlas: there are so many roads

under repair, roads closed,
no longer paths but culs-de-sac.

So we begin like a god by giving streets
the names of trees, then rivers, then cities
in other countries. We name the universe
of the body: start here, your hair dark as Mytilini

olives, shot with silver spark; your nipples
salmon cast and your clavicle a bridge
that moves me to the route
of sable hair down your belly.

If my tongue were a highlighter
you'd be lit up like a metropolis at midnight.
You taste like copper coins, sea salt, peaches and bigarreau.
You taste like you know where you're going.

You taste like indecision and desire, like a fire
reddening the edges of an orchard; you taste like Spain,
siestas and canella, girls with white skirts flaring in the wind.
You taste like travel: the inherent promise of maps.

Eating Olives in the House of Heartbroken Women

My sister leans against the stove, nibbling
olives. Like a Rossetti painting she is pure
mischief and melancholy. She is not me,
but she is part of me. She is everything,
and nothing. She is flesh,
and fault. Part solitude, part
social like an ocean with boats
bobbing on it. Her face so sad it breaks
plates, the floor littered with pits and tears.

We eat elitses, the sweet Crete varietal;
atalanti, purple-green and plump;
spanish olives stuffed with pimentos—*dragon eyes*
we call them. Small orbs tasting
of oceans and distance. Picking olives
on the Turkish countryside years ago
is the closest we've come to religion.

My sister is backlit from the open window
unaware of her loveliness. The only
sound, the chew of fruit.
Faith is in small things, she says
passing me the jar that smells
of creosote and roses.

Outside, the sky spirals in a pink
froth. Here we are. Her face.
My face. In this kitchen the light
has a sharpness that makes our eyes ache
as we watch the cat stalk a cardinal
across the yard. We are bone,
and break. There is a country

in my stomach as the sun
honeycombs through the screen.
In this house of heartbroken women,
two girls lean into the light, spitting pits,
learning the difference between sanctuary and salvation.

Acknowledgments

Grateful acknowledgment is made to the editors of the following magazines and anthologies in which these poems first appeared:

Amaranth: "Letters to a Lover from Another Planet."
America: "There Is a Word for It."
Black River Review: "The Air Lost in Breathing."
Bloomsbury Review: "Eating Honeybuns on the Louisiana Highway."
Bottomfish: "Negative."
Calyx: A Journal of Art and Literature by Women: "Arizona."
The Comstock Review: "Your Limbs Are Knotted Ropes," "Bone-flower."
Crab Orchard Review: "Desire Takes a Road Trip to New Orleans."
Fish Stories Collective: "Branches" and "When We Breathe."
Glimmer Train's Poetry Presentation: "Eating Olives in the House of Heartbroken Women."
Hammers: "The Fix-It Man," and "Tom Waits, I Hate You."
Jackleg: "On Hearing My Father Pulled a Shotgun. . ." and "Letters to a Lover. . ."
Louisiana Literature: "Walking," "Insomnia," and "Open Letter to Eros."
Many Mountains Moving: "Desire's Exhalations and Incidentals of Happiness."
Maryland Poetry Review: "It is the Cloud-Shingled Sky That Sends Me Back to You."
Notre Dame Review: "Toledo Bend"
Onionhead Literary Quarterly: "Bellpeppers."
Potpourri: "The Body's Migration."
Primavera: "Blackberries."
Rattapallax: "Finale for a Girl in a Skirt Sewn of Sky" and "Sin."
Red Brick Review: "The Problem with Celibacy."
River Oak Review: "Girls Gathered for a High School Photo, Circa 1960."
Sandhills Review: "Inflorescence."
Sniper Logic: "Denali Highway."
Strong Coffee: "His Black Scrawl."
Southern Poetry Review: "Reading Ed Ochester on the Plane from Chicago to Denver."
Sundog: "The Etiquette of Shells."
Swerve: "It is in this field" and "Love Travels in the Pockets of Old Men."
Willow Springs: "Loneliness."

"Finale for a Girl in a Skirt Sewn of Sky" and "Eating Olives in the House of Heartbroken Women" were compiled in the *Gazelle Poets Anthology*. "Red Dress" appeared in *Powerlines: The Chicago Guild Complex's 10-year anthology*. "Bone-flower" was published in *Rising to the Dawn Anthology*. An earlier version of this manuscript received the Harcourt, Brace & Jovanovich Award for Poetry. A section of this book called *Love's Apostrophes* won the Sheila-Na-Gig 1998 Poetry Chapbook Contest. "When We Breathe" received an Illinois Arts Council Award.

ABOUT THE AUTHOR

Simone Muench is the associate editor of ACM (*Another Chicago Magazine*). She was raised in Benson, Louisiana, and the Ozark Mountains in Combs, Arkansas, before moving to Colorado to receive her B.A. and M.A. from the University of Colorado. Her manuscript "Love's Apostrophes" won the 1998 Sheila-Na-Gig Chapbook Contest. She recently was a recipient of an Illinois Arts Council Fellowship. She resides in Chicago where she waits tables at the United Center for Bulls and Blackhawks games and at Wrigley Field for the Cubs, even though she remains sports illiterate. *The Air Lost in Breathing* is her first book.

Other Books by Helicon Nine Editions

FICTION

Toy Guns, a first collection of stories by Lisa Norris. Winner of the 1999 Willa Cather Fiction Prize. Selected by Al Young.

One Girl, a novel in stories by Sheila Kohler. Winner of the 1998 Willa Cather Fiction Prize. Selected by William Gass.

Climbing the God Tree, a novel in stories by Jaimee Wriston Colbert. 1997 Willa Cather Fiction Prizewinner. Selected by Dawn Raffel.

Eternal City, a first collection of stories by Molly Shapiro. Winner of the 1996 Willa Cather Fiction Prize. Selected by Hilary Masters.

Knucklebones, 27 short stories by Annabel Thomas. 1994 Willa Cather Fiction Prizewinner. Selected by Daniel Stern.

Galaxy Girls:Wonder Women, stories by Anne Whitney Pierce. 1993 Willa Cather Fiction Prizewinner. Selected by Carolyn Doty.

Return to Sender, a first novel by Ann Slegman.

The Value of Kindness, short stories by Ellyn Bache, 1992 Willa Cather Fiction Prizewinner. Selected by James Byron Hall.

Italian Smoking Piece with Simultaneous Translation, by Christy Sheffield-Sanford. A multi-dimensional tour de force.

Sweet Angel Band, a first book of stories by Rose Marie Kinder. 1991 Willa Cather Fiction Prizewinner. Selected by Robley Wilson.

POETRY

Flesh, a first book of poems by Susan Gubernat. Winner of the 1998 Marianne Moore Poetry Prize. Selected by Robert Phillips.

Diasporadic, a first book of poems by Patty Seyburn. Winner of the 1997 Marianne Moore Poetry Prize. Selected by Molly Peacock. Received the 2000 Notable Book Award for Poetry (American Library Association).

On Days Like This, poems about baseball and life by the late Dan Quisenberry., one of America's favorite pitchers.

Prayers to the Other Life, a first book of poems by Christopher Seid. Winner of the 1996 Marianne Moore Poetry Prize. Selected by David Ray.

A Strange Heart, a second book of poems by Jane O. Wayne. Winner of the 1995 Marianne Moore Poetry Prize. Selected by James Tate. Received the 1996 Society of Midland Authors Poetry Competition Award.

Without Warning, a second book of poems by Elizabeth Goldring. Co-published with BkMk Press, University of Missouri-Kansas City.

Night Drawings, a first book of poems by Marjorie Stelmach. Winner of the 1994 Marianne Moore Poetry Prize. Introduction by David Ignatow, judge.

Wool Highways, poems of New Zealand by David Ray. Winner of the 1993 William Carlos Williams Poetry Award (Poetry Society of America).

My Journey Toward You, a first book of poems by Judy Longley. Winner of the 1993 Marianne Moore Poetry Prize. Introduction by Richard Howard, judge.

Women in Cars, a first book of poems by Martha McFerren. Winner of the 1992 Marianne Moore Poetry Prize. Introduction by Colette Inez, judge.

Hoofbeats on the Door, a first book of poems by Regina deCormier. Introduction by Richard Howard.

Black Method, a first book of poems by Biff Russ. Winner of the 1991 Marianne Moore Poetry Prize. Introduction by Mona Van Duyn, judge.

ANTHOLOGIES

Spud Songs: An Anthology of Potato Poems, edited by Gloria Vando and Robert Stewart. Proceeds to benefit Hunger Relief.

Poets at Large: 25 Poets in 25 Homes, edited by H.L. Hix. A gathering of 25 poets in Kansas City commemorating National Poetry Month.

The Helicon Nine Reader: A Celebration of Women in the Arts., edited by Gloria Vando Hickok. The best of ten years of *Helicon Nine: The Journal of Women's Arts & Letters*.

FEUILLETS

Limited editions of little books, ranging in length from 4–24 pages, accompanied by a mailing envelope.

Ancient Musics, a poetry sequence by Albert Goldbarth.

A Walk through the Human Heart, a poem by Robley Wilson.

Christmas 1956, a poem by Keith Denniston.

Climatron, a poem by Robert Stewart.

Cortége, a poem by Carl Phillips.

Down & In, poems by Dan Quisenberry.

Dresden, a poem by Patricia Cleary Miller.

Generations, a poem by George Wedge.

The Heart, a short story by Catherine Browder.

R. I. P., a poem by E.S. Miller.

Short Prose, an illustrated essay by M. Kasper.

Slivers, a poem by Philip Miller.

Stravinsky's Dream, a story by Conger Beasley, Jr.

This is how they were placed for us, a poem by Luci Tapahonso.

Tokens, a poem by Judy Ray.